S0-AJP-928

COMPARABLES

by Bill Jeakle and Ed Wyatt

Andrews and McMeel
A Universal Press Syndicate Company
Kansas City

Comparables copyright © 1992 by Bill Jeakle and Ed Wyatt. All rights reserved. Printed in the United States of America. No part of this book may be used or reproduced in any manner whatsoever without written permission except in the case of reprints in the context of reviews. For information write Andrews and McMeel, a Universal Press Syndicate Company, 4900 Main Street, Kansas City, Missouri 64112.

Library of Congress Cataloging-in-Publication Data

Jeakle, Bill.
    Comparables / by Bill Jeakle and Ed Wyatt.
       p.   cm.
    ISBN 0-8362-7995-6 (pbk.) : $6.95
    1. Word games. I. Wyatt, Ed. II. Title.
    GV1507.W8J43   1992   92-4438
    793.73—dc20   CIP

Illustrated and designed by Barrie Maguire

────── **Attention: Schools and Businesses** ──────

Andrews and McMeel books are available at quantity discounts with bulk purchase for educational, business, or sales promotional use. For information, please write to: Special Sales Department, Andrews and McMeel, 4900 Main Street, Kansas City, Missouri 64112.

For Joe Piscatella

Sincere Acknowledgments **or** Sycophantic Flattery

The authors wish to thank the following people for their help in the process of producing *Comparables:* Everyone at "Almost Live!," especially Bill Stainton, Bill Nye, and Steve Wilson. KING-TV's Kirk Shroeder, Willie McClarron, and Walt McGinn for bringing them to life on TV. John Maynard at KXRX, Kit Boss, Joe Guppy, Mary Schetter at Turner Broadcasting, Dave Hill, Steve Nieswander, Brad Peterson, Romney Wyatt, and the Happy Mondays. Special thanks go to the people we worked with at Andrews and McMeel: Tom Thornton, Donna Martin, Dorothy O'Brien, and our editor Kathy Holder.

1. Legal Term **or** Roman Leader
   A. Marcus Aurelius
   B. Habeas Corpus
   C. Caius Ligarious
   D. Writ of Mandamus

2. Polaroid Camera or **Famous Person's Horse**
   A. Pronto
   B. Silver
   C. One-Step
   D. Trigger

3. Olympic Athlete **or** Meaningless Phrase
    A. Ferd Brek
    B. Gerd Bonk
    C. Ard Schenck
    D. Parv Melk

4. **Radical Political Group** or **"Twin Peaks" Co-Star**
    A. **Sinn Fein**
    B. **Madchen Amick**
    C. **Sherilyn Fenn**
    D. **Bader Meinhoff**

5. Historical Figure **or** Tennis Pro
   A. Christo Van Rensberg
   B. Anton van Leeuwenhoek
   C. Vasco da Gama
   D. Carl Uwe Steeb

6. British Soccer Team or **Eclectic Car**
   A. Morris Minor
   B. Aston Villa
   C. Nash Metropolitan
   D. Tottenham Hotspur

7. Complimentary Adjective **or** Ancient Pope
   A. Beneficent
   B. Boniface
   C. Pius
   D. Devout

8. Fashion Model or **Small Nation in the Middle East**
   A. Oman
   B. Yasmine
   C. Iman
   D. Yemen

9. X-Rated Performer **or** Tasty Cookie
   A. Ginger Lynn
   B. Lorna Doone
   C. Ginger Snap
   D. Melissa Mounds

10. Baseball Hall of Famer or **Expensive Dinner**
A. Rabbit Maranville
B. Vitello Medallion
C. Napoleon Lajoie
D. Shrimp Scampi

11. Basketball Slang **or** British Verb
A. Hoover
B. Hooper
C. Hoosier
D. Haver

12. Biblical Figure or **County in Utah**
    A. Juab
    B. Haggai
    C. Uintah
    D. Og

13. Chewing Tobacco **or** Thing You Do With Your Nose
    A. Snuff
    B. Snort
    C. Sniff
    D. Snoose

14. French Wine or **Hockey Player**
    A. Lemieux
    B. Bordeaux
    C. Robitaille
    D. Merlot

15. Mass Murderer **or** Sitcom Neighbor
    A. Howard Borden
    B. Richard Speck
    C. Charles Whitman
    D. Fred Mertz

16. **Wrestling Term** or **Stage of the Moon**
    A. **Full Nelson**
    B. **Waning Crescent**
    C. **Gibbous**
    D. **Figure Four**

17. Type of Rock **or** Unflattering Adjective
    A. Igneous
    B. Unctuous
    C. Supercilious
    D. Gneiss

18. Famous Spy or **Sound You Make When You're Out of Breath**
    A. Hiss
    B. Huff
    C. Hale
    D. Hooph

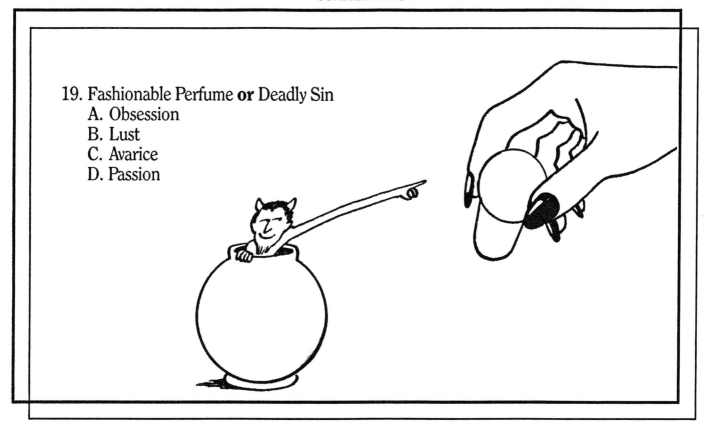

19. Fashionable Perfume **or** Deadly Sin
    A. Obsession
    B. Lust
    C. Avarice
    D. Passion

20. Fancy Hotel or **Prep School Cheerleader**
   A. Ashley Fairmont
   B. Rosslyn Westpark
   C. Beverly Wilshire
   D. Britney Canfield

21. Gum Disease **or** Lithuanian Basketball Star
   A. Kurtainaitas
   B. Periodontitis
   C. Gingivitis
   D. Marciulionis

22. Exotic Dish or **African City**
   A. Mogadiscio
   B. Felafel
   C. Accra
   D. Babaganoosh

23. European Coin **or** Nonsensical Gibberish
   A. Mep
   B. Lek
   C. Logul
   D. Forint

24. Kool-Aid Character or **Baseball Great**
   A. Lefty Lemon
   B. Lefty Grove
   C. Pepper Martin
   D. Goofy Grape

25. Eastern European Car **or** Game Show Host

   A. Trabant
   B. Trebeck
   C. Lada
   D. Sajak

26. **Japanese Food** or **Southern Woman's Action**

   A. Sashay
   B. Sashimi
   C. Sushi
   D. Curtsy

27. Typographical Error **or** Town in Wales
    A. Llwyngwril
    B. Ub Stwuffl
    C. Cwm Ystwyth
    D. Llutzwln

28. Defense Acronym or **Junior High Putdown**
    A. Norad
    B. Geek
    C. Awacs
    D. Dweeb

29. European Province **or** Little Gift
  A. Lagniappe
  B. Anjou
  C. Tchotchke
  D. Kamchatka

30. Famous Composer or **Type of Noodle**
  A. Puccini
  B. Rotini
  C. Verdi
  D. Mostaccioli

31. High-Powered Alcohol **or** Tennis Term
  A. Rotgut
  B. Catgut
  C. Eight Ball
  D. Poach

32. College Football Team or **Thing in the Ocean**
   A. Red Tide
   B. Crimson Tide
   C. Green Wave
   D. Blue Crab

33. Romantic Poet **or** Cracker
   A. Wheatsworth
   B. Keats
   C. Coleridge
   D. Ritz

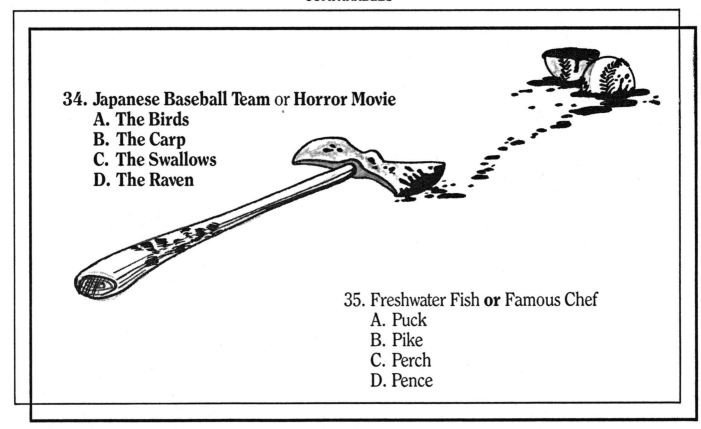

34. Japanese Baseball Team or **Horror Movie**
   A. The Birds
   B. The Carp
   C. The Swallows
   D. The Raven

35. Freshwater Fish **or** Famous Chef
   A. Puck
   B. Pike
   C. Perch
   D. Pence

36. Trendy Ad Agency or **Soul Singing Group**
   A. Babbit and Reiman
   B. Ashford and Simpson
   C. Wieden and Kennedy
   D. Peaches and Herb

37. Baby Talk **or** Food Mart
   A. Wa Wa
   B. Goo Goo
   C. Dabby Dooby
   D. Piggly Wiggly

38. Musical Term or **Obscure African Country**
   A. Basso Profundo
   B. Burkina Faso
   C. Arioso
   D. Togo

39. Southern Basketball Player **or** *Jabberwocky* Character
   A. Litterial Green
   B. Jubjub Bird
   C. Locksley Collie
   D. Frumious Bandersnatch

40. Female Singer or **Tropical Island**
   A. Captiva
   B. Martika
   C. Basia
   D. Mustique

41. Comic Strip Character **or** Football Coach
   A. Duffy Daugherty
   B. Snuffy Smith
   C. Beetle Bailey
   D. Spike Dykes

42. Cajun Food or **Reggae Terminology**
   A. Roux
   B. Jah
   C. Ire
   D. Etouffée

43. King Arthur Character **or** Cure for Baldness
    A. Igraine
    B. Rogaine
    C. Modred
    D. Wig

44. Pop/Rock Band or **Cute Little Movie**
    A. The Beautiful South
    B. The Unbelievable Truth
    C. The Tragically Hip
    D. The Sure Thing

45. Legal Precedent **or** Championship Prizefight
    A. Roe vs. Wade
    B. Baker vs. Carr
    C. Dempsey vs. Carpentier
    D. Kilrain vs. Sullivan

46. Ecuadorian City or **Lottery Game**
    A. Quito
    B. Quinto
    C. Wingo
    D. Lago

47. News Reporter **or** New Jersey Waterway
    A. Arthur Kill
    B. Van Earl Wright
    C. Arthur Kent
    D. Kill Van Kull

48. Reagan Cabinet Member or **Town in Oregon**
    A. Milton Freewater
    B. Malcolm Baldridge
    C. Milton Friedman
    D. John Day

49. Town in Maine **or** Midwest Farm Crop
    A. Lubec
    B. Sorghum
    C. Orono
    D. Milo

50. Ski Area or **Superstitious Religion**
    A. Juju
    B. Hoodoo
    C. Voodoo
    D. Okemo

51. Washington Place Name **or** Exhortation to a Friend
    A. Skookumchuck
    B. Getemrick
    C. Chuckanut
    D. Stophimnow

52. Rap Star or **Type of Gum**
    A. Flavor Flav
    B. Plen T Pak
    C. Care Free
    D. Easy E

53. Baseball Pitcher's Nickname **or** Comment Before Sex
    A. Big Unit
    B. Wow
    C. Eck
    D. Ha Ha

54. Eastern Oregon Town or **Way to Prevent Disease**
    A. Condon
    B. Bleach
    C. Spray
    D. Pill

55. Music Group **or** Northwest Landmark
    A. Rooster Rock
    B. Point No Point
    C. No Means No
    D. Was (Not Was)

56. Rock Band or **Woman's Dilemma**
    A. Jane's Addiction
    B. Karen's Parents
    C. Alice in Chains
    D. Susie Under Water

57. Publishing House **or** Exit off Interstate 5
    A. Ankeny Hill
    B. Harper Collins
    C. Vader Ryderwood
    D. Addison Wesley

58. Hawaiian Food or **Skinhead Slang**
    A. Poi
    B. Oi
    C. Lau Lau
    D. Wanker

59. Mexican Food Entrée **or** Suburb of L.A.
    A. Quesadilla
    B. Encino
    C. Cucamonga
    D. Flauta

60. European Motorcycle or **Hardcore Band**
    A. Ducati
    B. Fugazi
    C. Moto Guzzi
    D. Motorhead

61. Blonde Actress **or** Obscure Sport
    A. Scacchi
    B. Bocce
    C. Berte
    D. Jarts

62. Jazz Great or **Human Condition**
    A. Encephalomyelitis
    B. Thelonius
    C. Marsalis
    D. Homunculus

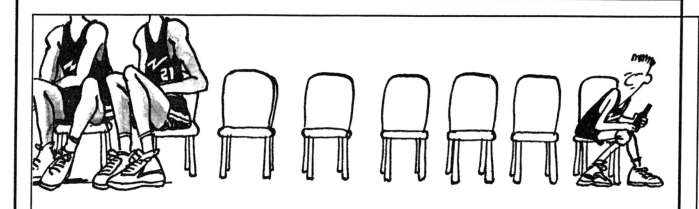

63. Type of Beer **or** Marginal NBA Guard
    A. Haffner
    B. Pilsner
    C. Porter
    D. Tucker

64. Asian Company or **Caffeinated Beverage**
   A. Lotte
   B. Mocha
   C. Pekoe
   D. Seibu

65. European Soccer Team **or** Character From *The Odyssey*
   A. Ajax
   B. Telemachus
   C. Juventus
   D. Laertes

66. College Mascot or **Electronics Manufacturer**
   A. Saluki
   B. Sansui
   C. Aiwa
   D. Hoya

67. British Prep School **or** Thing on a Farm
   A. Harrow
   B. Fallow
   C. Charterhouse
   D. Windrow

68. Austrian Tennis Player or **Type of Spice**
   A. Tarragon
   B. Muster
   C. Skorff
   D. Fennel

69. Western Oil Company **or** Pornographic Filmmakers
    A. Leathers
    B. Dark Brothers
    C. Caballero
    D. Awful Brothers

70. Imported 4-Wheel-Drive Vehicle or **Bruce Willis's Kid**
   A. Scout
   B. Rocky
   C. Rumer
   D. Justy

71. Revolutionary Leader **or** Type of Volkswagen
   A. Marat
   B. Guevara
   C. Corrado
   D. Passat

72. Sports Arena or **Economical Car**
    A. Summit
    B. Horizon
    C. Scope
    D. Scoupe

73. NBA Team from Florida **or** Public Utility
    A. Light
    B. Heat
    C. Magic
    D. Sewer

74. Non-Alcoholic Beer or **Handgun**
    A. Buckler
    B. Kaliber
    C. Derringer
    D. Glock

75. "Hogan's Heroes" Actor **or** Small Bird
    A. Kestrel
    B. Klemperer
    C. Merganser
    D. Crane

76. Secret Society Leader or **Grateful Dead Song**
    A. Estimated Prophet
    B. Worshipful Master
    C. Kleagle
    D. Ripple

77. Household Object **or** Thing from "Star Trek"
    A. Trivet
    B. Tribble
    C. Romulan
    D. Ottoman

78. Country Band or **Canadian Beer**
   A. Wild Rose
   B. O'Keefes
   C. Kokanee
   D. O'Kanes

79. Catholic Phrase **or** Town in Texas
   A. Mea Culpa
   B. Corpus Christi
   C. Hail Mary
   D. Hale Center

80. Rock Group or **Venereal Disease**
   A. The Clap
   B. The Snap
   C. The Crabs
   D. The Flamin' Groovies

81. Sitcom Actress **or** Type of Tractor
  A. Harley Kozak
  B. Allis Chalmers
  C. Allyce Beasley
  D. Massey Ferguson

82. Old-Timer Baseball Team or **What Kids Want to Be When They Grow Up**
  A. Farmers
  B. Millers
  C. Exporters
  D. Doctors

83. Daily Newspaper **or** Colloquial Praise
    A. Plain Dealer
    B. Straight Shooter
    C. Stalwart
    D. Statesman

84. **Military Acronym** or **Talk Show Hosts**
    A. **Sams**
    B. **Sallys**
    C. **Johnnys**
    D. **Mirvs**

85. Techno-Dance Band **or** Problem With Your Body
    A. Nine Inch Nails
    B. Smashed Fingers
    C. Ripped Flesh
    D. Severed Heads

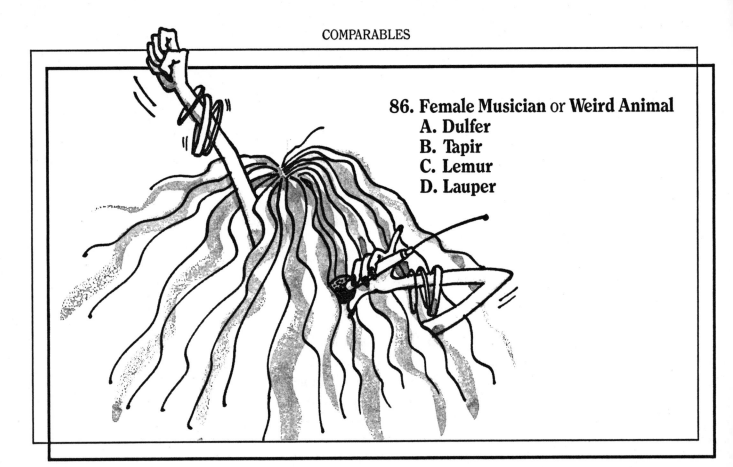

86. Female Musician or **Weird Animal**
    A. Dulfer
    B. Tapir
    C. Lemur
    D. Lauper

87. Minneapolis Suburb **or** Yiddish Word
    A. Chaska
    B. Shiksa
    C. Edina
    D. Goy

88. Baseball Pitcher or **Method of Cleaning**
A. Bream
B. Dibble
C. Burba
D. Scour

89. Term from Eastern Philosophy **or** Babe from Brazil
    A. Xuxa
    B. Braga
    C. Shuha
    D. Raga

90. Mythical Bird or **Young Actress**
    A. Griffin
    B. Kensit
    C. Ryder
    D. Phoenix

91. European Sports Term **or** Slang for Getting Sick
    A. Korf
    B. Toss
    C. Hurl
    D. Blow

92. German Writer or **Type of Grain**
    A. Groat
    B. Goethe
    C. Grist
    D. Grass

93. Big City High School **or** Term for People
    A. Male
    B. Guys
    C. Girls
    D. Kid

94. Movie Sound System or **Type of Cheese**
    A. Foley
    B. Colby
    C. Dolby
    D. Jack

95. Type of Candy **or** Thing in Your Nose
    A. Altoid
    B. Adenoid
    C. Septum
    D. Dots

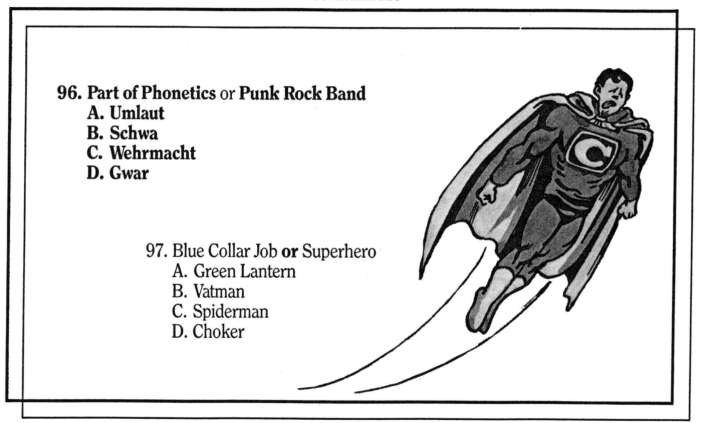

96. Part of Phonetics or **Punk Rock Band**
   A. Umlaut
   B. Schwa
   C. Wehrmacht
   D. Gwar

97. Blue Collar Job **or** Superhero
   A. Green Lantern
   B. Vatman
   C. Spiderman
   D. Choker

98. Surfer Term or **Thing That Gets Hammered**
   A. Rad
   B. Trig
   C. Shim
   D. Dude

99. European Food **or** Former Member of The Clash
   A. Strummer
   B. Banger
   C. Topper
   D. Kipper

100. Old TV Show or **Unlikely Pairing**
   A. The Ghost and Mrs. Muir
   B. The Lion and Mrs. Wilson
   C. The Scarecrow and Mrs. King
   D. The Transmission and Mrs. Chilcutt

101. Hot Music Performer **or** Thing in a Pickup Truck
   A. Hammer
   B. Cable
   C. Axl
   D. Gear

102. Summer Olympic Site or **Bland American Car**
   A. Sapporo
   B. Athens
   C. Melbourne
   D. Bonneville

103. Finnish Hockey Star **or** Indian Food
  A. Kurri
  B. Korma
  C. Tikkanen
  D. Samosa

104. Country Singers or **Dirty Magazine**
    A. Judds
    B. Juggs
    C. Sweethearts of the Rodeo
    D. Busty Beauties

105. Baseball Legend **or** Rural Landmark
    A. Jumpoff Joe Creek
    B. Smoky Joe Wood
    C. Great Slave Lake
    D. Dizzy Trout

106. Small College or **Declaration of Independence Signer**
  A. Johnson C. Smith
  B. Button Gwinnett
  C. Charles Carroll
  D. Gustavus Adolphus

107. Tasty Flavoring **or** Woman You Might Know
  A. Molly McButter
  B. Betty O'Pepper
  C. Ms. Charcoal
  D. Mrs. Dash

108. Microsoft Program or **Street Lingo**
   A. Word
   B. Def
   C. Fresh
   D. Excel

109. Baseball Error **or** Preppy Shoemaker
   A. Bean
   B. Boot
   C. Bass
   D. Botch

110. African Nation or **New Age Musician**
   A. Yanni
   B. Gabon
   C. Zamfir
   D. Chad

111. Canadian Football League Team **or** Type of Prophylactic
    A. Trojans
    B. Roughriders
    C. Blue Bombers
    D. Skins

112. Telephone Service or **Type of Mazda**
    A. 929
    B. 911
    C. 626
    D. 411

113. Mutual Fund **or** English Car
    A. Vanguard Windsor
    B. Vauxhall Carlton
    C. Fidelity Magellan
    D. Aston Martin

114. Model of Hyundai or **Psychological Complex**
    A. Elantra
    B. Electra
    C. Sonata
    D. Oedipus

115. Famous Builder **or** Regional Beer
    A. Roebling
    B. Yuengling
    C. Gablinger
    D. Bartholdi

116. Town in Canada or **Obscure President**
    A. Hamilton
    B. Pierce
    C. Emerson
    D. Arthur

117. Repressive Family Law **or** Creepy TV Character
 A. Jim Crow
 B. Grandpa
 C. Grandfather
 D. Uncle Fester

118. Eastern European Nationality or **Chess Maneuver**
 A. Magyar
 B. Zugzwang
 C. Slovak
 D. Check

119. Type of Drink **or** Old-Time King
 A. Zog
 B. Gog
 C. Grog
 D. Nog

120. Federal League Baseball Team or **Cigar**
    A. Stogies
    B. Peps
    C. Havanas
    D. Sweets

121. Fairy Tale Character **or** Fascist American Leader
    A. Prince
    B. Duke
    C. Butler
    D. Witch

122. Baltic Capital or **Actress With Swedish Name**
    A. Riga
    B. Lena
    C. Tallinn
    D. Uma

123. First Lady **or** Itinerant Entertainer
    A. Betty
    B. Carnie
    C. Mamie
    D. Mime

124. Monopoly Property or **U2 Song**
    A. Water Works
    B. Electric Co.
    C. Van Diemen's Land
    D. Marvin Gardens

125. Obscure Foreign Capital **or** Expression of Frustration
    A. Uff Da
    B. Ulan Bator
    C. Sacre Bleu
    D. Godthaab

126. Underground Band or **Kids' Cereal**
  A. Dinosaur Jr.
  B. Frankenberry
  C. Crispy Critters
  D. Wonderstuff

127. Unflattering Putdown **or** Slang for Home Run
  A. Slacker
  B. Dinger
  C. Tater
  D. Cracker

128. Notre Dame Coach or **Pesky Bug**
  A. Chigger
  B. Digger
  C. Gipper
  D. Skeeter

129. Sports Fans Action **or** Pro Wrestling Move
    A. The Tomahawk Chop
    B. The Atomic Drop
    C. The Wave
    D. The Heart Punch

130. Idaho Landmark or **Regional Soft Drink**
   A. Shasta
   B. Sun Valley
   C. Green River
   D. Sawtooth

131. Animal Young **or** *Great Expectations* Character
   A. Kit
   B. Pirrip
   C. Squab
   D. Trabb

132. Psychiatric Term or **Soviet Coup Plotter**
   A. Yazov
   B. Rorschach
   C. Yanayev
   D. Pavlov

133. Crime Duo **or** Retail Store
   A. Abercrombie and Fitch
   B. Sacco and Vanzetti
   C. Leopold and Loeb
   D. Crabtree and Evelyn

134. Faulkner Hero or **Disease**
   A. Snopes
   B. Scabies
   C. Compson
   D. Graves

135. *Great Gatsby* Character **or** Presidential Appointee
   A. Jordan Baker
   B. Paul Volker
   C. Meyer Wolfsheim
   D. Howard Baker

136. Famous Ascetics or **Cartoon**
   A. Abélard and Héloise
   B. Hi and Lois
   C. Duns Scotus
   D. The Fusco Brothers

137. Children's TV Comedy Food **or** Foreign Spreadable Substance
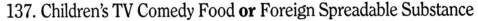
    A. Vegemite
    B. Scooby Snack
    C. Nutella
    D. Green Slime

138. Cellist's First Name or **Toy**
    A. Yo Yo
    B. Slinky
    C. Pablo
    D. Gumby

139. Desert Name **or** Exotic Coffee
  A. Gobi
  B. Sumatra
  C. Mojave
  D. Kona

140. Good Move in Volleyball or **Violent Move in Seal Hunting**
  A. Smash
  B. Club
  C. Kill
  D. Clobber

141. Ancient Navigational Tool **or** Sex Toy
     A. Astrolabe
     B. St. James Cross
     C. Sextant
     D. Ben Wa Balls

142. Military Weapon Prefix or **James Cameron-Directed Movie**
     A. Terminator
     B. M1A1
     C. T2
     D. Harrier

143. Defunct Magazine **or** Admired Trait
    A. Chutzpah
    B. Fame
    C. Pep
    D. Moxie

144. Andy Griffith Character or **Johnny Carson Creation**
    A. Earnest T. Bass
    B. Aunt Blabby
    C. Floyd R. Turbo
    D. Aunt Bee

145. Space Shuttle **or** Admirable Trait
    A. Discovery
    B. Enterprise
    C. Courage
    D. Wherewithal

146. J. D. Salinger Character or **Don Johnson/Melanie Griffith Kid**
    A. Zooey
    B. Dakota
    C. Jesse
    D. Holden

147. Columbus Ship **or** Bean
   A. Pinto
   B. Nina
   C. Lima
   D. Pinta

148. Nautical Term or **Naughty Teenage Game**
   A. Spin the Bottle
   B. Jibber the Kibber
   C. Hard to Port
   D. Submarine Races

149. Part of the Eye **or** Italian Restaurant in New York
   A. Sclera
   B. Retina
   C. Sfuzzi
   D. Leoni

150. New York Disco or **Periodic Table Element**
   A. Palladium
   B. Limelight
   C. Mars
   D. Xenon

151. Stage of the Moon **or** Household Chore
    A. Waning
    B. Washing
    C. Waxing
    D. Wiping

152. Geological Epoch or **Word Used to Describe a Person Who Has Had Substantial Plastic Surgery**
    A. Eocene
    B. Pleistocene
    C. Obscene
    D. Polythene

153. Small Bird **or** Boorish Person
    A. Plodder
    B. Plover
    C. Puffin
    D. Buffoon

154. Yemini Currency or **Indian Guy Associated with The Beatles**
    A. Riyal
    B. Ravi
    C. Bugshah
    D. Mahesh

155. Recipient of Letters from the Apostle Paul **or** Skin Problem
    A. Thessylonians
    B. Lesions
    C. Ephesians
    D. Bunions

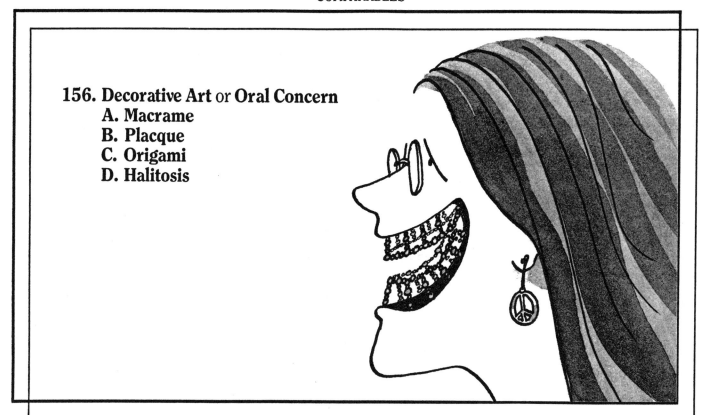

156. Decorative Art or **Oral Concern**
  A. Macrame
  B. Placque
  C. Origami
  D. Halitosis

157. Greek Architectural Term **or** Part of the Foot
  A. Ionic
  B. Arch
  C. Taursus
  D. Plinth

158. Greek Letter or **Movie Theater Chain**
  A. Omicron
  B. Odeon
  C. Paramount
  D. Omega

159. Hebrew Letter **or** Foster Brooks's Drunk Imitation
    A. Shtuff
    B. Zayin
    C. Ocifer
    D. Resh

160. Arabic Letter or **Gomer Pyle Expression**
    A. Gaw
    B. Waw
    C. Dal
    D. Gol

161. City in Albania **or** Fleetwood Mac Song
    A. Tirana
    B. Rhiannon
    C. Tusk
    D. Fier

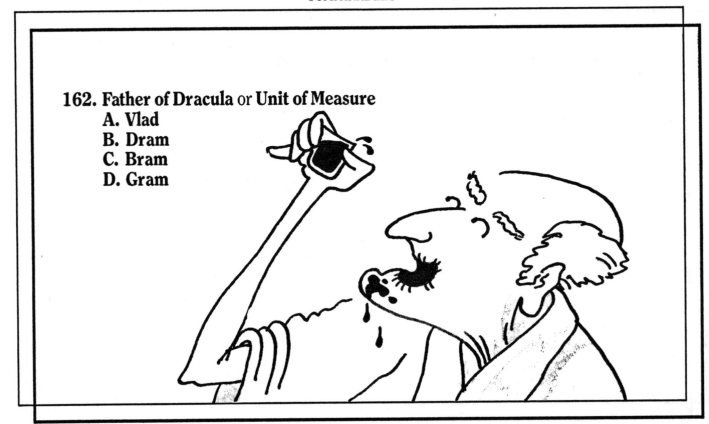

162. **Father of Dracula** or **Unit of Measure**
 A. Vlad
 B. Dram
 C. Bram
 D. Gram

163. Explorer **or** Single Frame Comic Strip
    A. Pizarro
    B. Marmaduke
    C. Drake
    D. Guindon

164. Governmental Term or Piece of Furniture
    A. Hutch
    B. Speaker
    C. Loveseat
    D. Chair

165. Private College **or** Former British Prime Minister
    A. Pitt
    B. Hollins
    C. Heath
    D. Hahnemann

166. US Dam or **Heisman Trophy Winner**
    A. Dworshak
    B. Hart
    C. Swift
    D. Griffin

167. Goofy Acronym **or** Lewis Carroll Invention
    A. Nimby
    B. Jabberwock
    C. Snafu
    D. Chortle

168. Rapid Transit System or **Character from "The Simpsons"**
   A. Marta
   B. Marge
   C. Max
   D. Homer

169. Bird **or** Old Saturday Morning Show
   A. Archie
   B. Jay
   C. Robin
   D. Shazam

170. Automatic Teller or **Clue Character**
  A. Tillie
  B. Miss Peacock
  C. Colonel Mustard
  D. Mr. Moneybags

171. Kosher Food Term **or** Game
  A. Oh-Wah-Ree
  B. Matzoh
  C. Yahtzee
  D. Gefelte

172. National Park or **Golf Hazard**
  A. Flaming Gorge
  B. Casual Water
  C. Badlands
  D. Ground Under Repair

173. Type of Sport **or** What You Would Be Doing If You Fell Off a Cliff
    A. Curling
    B. Flailing
    C. Tumbling
    D. Screaming

174. Hockey Division or **Revolutionary War Patriot**
- **A. Patrick**
- **B. Hancock**
- **C. Smythe**
- **D. Henry**

175. Horse Racing Stakes **or** Fairy Tale
- A. Mother Goose
- B. Jack Sprat
- C. Spinster
- D. Hans Brinker

176. Severe Hurricane or **"Bewitched" Character**
- **A. Agnes**
- **B. Hugo**
- **C. Darren**
- **D. Gladys**

177. Satellite Transmission **or** R&B Group
    A. SOS Band
    B. KU Band
    C. Dazz Band
    D. C Band

178. Formula One Race Car Driver or **Home Entertainer**
    A. A. Prost
    B. M. Stewart
    C. T. Fabi
    D. N. Dupree

179. Athletic Conference **or** Meteorological Warning
    A. Big Sky
    B. Gathering Clouds
    C. Sunbelt
    D. Ice Storm

180. Singapore Government Official or **Sound You Make on a Roller Coaster**
    A. Wee
    B. Wah
    C. Yew
    D. Yow

181. Foreign Word for "Yes" **or** Baby's First Word
    A. Da
    B. Ga
    C. Ja
    D. Ba

182. Fishing Apparatus or **Dance**
A. Bob
B. Lindy
C. Jig
D. Bop

183. Labor Organization **or** Wrestling Federation
    A. IWW
    B. WWF
    C. IBEW
    D. NWA

184. Perry Mason Character or **Garden Implement**
    A. Trag
    B. Drake
    C. Trowel
    D. Spade

185. Old Time Movie Star **or** Housing Development
    A. Lillian Gish
    B. Chelsea Ridge
    C. Veronica Lane
    D. Tallulah Bankhead

186. Exotic Destination or **Rhythmic Movement**
    A. Salsa
    B. Rwanda
    C. Bamba
    D. Tonga

187. Mineral **or** Legal Term
    A. Nolo
    B. Antimony
    C. Bono
    D. Barite

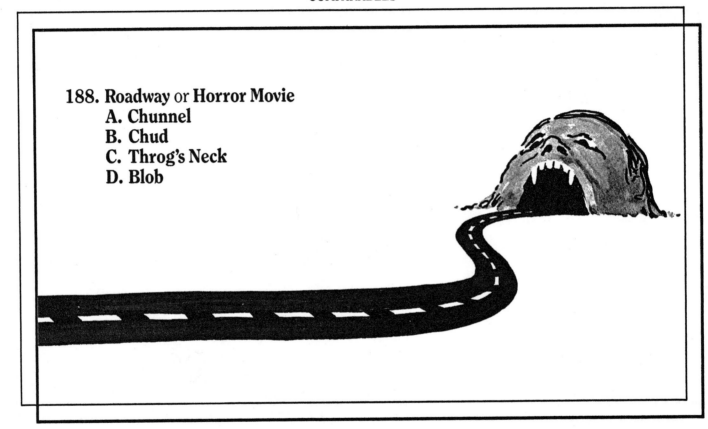

188. **Roadway** or **Horror Movie**
     A. **Chunnel**
     B. **Chud**
     C. **Throg's Neck**
     D. **Blob**

189. US Senator **or** Nerd's First Name
    A. Glenn
    B. Leonard
    C. Thurmond
    D. Herbert

190. UN Organization or **Defunct Shlock Band**
    A. Who
    B. Menudo
    C. Unido
    D. The Association

191. NPR Host **or** Bad TV Show
    A. Mara Liason
    B. Richard Brockleman
    C. Noah Adams
    D. Grizzly Adams

192. **Former US Vice President** or **Original Name of Hollywood Star**
    A. **Elbridge Gerry**
    B. **Archibald Leach**
    C. **William Henry Pratt**
    D. **Schuyler Colfax**

193. America's Cup Winner **or** How You'd Want Your Kids to Be
    A. Resolute
    B. Dutiful
    C. Vigilant
    D. Thrifty

194. State Motto or Beatles Lyric
    A. To be rather than to seem
    B. I'll follow the sun
    C. While I breathe, I hope
    D. To lead a better life

195. Collective of Animals **or** Item Found on a Police Report
    A. Grist
    B. Blood
    C. Murder
    D. Bullet

196. Former "Saturday Night Live" Performer or **Scientist**
 A. Francis Crick
 B. Charles Rocket
 C. Brad Hall
 D. Michael Faraday

197. Language Sect **or** Freudian Term
 A. Id
 B. Igbo
 C. Edo
 D. Libido

198. Foreign Airport or **Candy Bar**
 A. Orly
 B. Clark
 C. Heathrow
 D. Mars

199. Flower Part **or** Shakespeare's *Henry IV* Character
 A. Bardolf
 B. Pistil
 C. Falstaff
 D. Stamen

200. Endangered Species or **Social Undesirable**
 A. **Wild Yak**
 B. **Wild Man**
 C. **Wild Ass**
 D. **Party Animal**

COMPARABLES Answers

1. B and D could make an appearance in a courtroom. A and C, unfortunately, are dead.
2. **You wouldn't want to put your eye up to B or D and say "cheese."**
3. A and D never won an Olympic medal, in fact, they don't exist.
4. **B and C have probably never claimed responsibility for an illegal subversive action.**
5. If you want an easy win on the tennis court, you'd want to schedule a match against B or C.
6. **It would be quite a sight to see A or C kick a ball toward a goal.**
7. Good Catholics try to be A and D, and have respect for B and C.
8. **Finding a dress large enough to fit A and D would be impossible.**
9. A or D wouldn't be appropriate for your kid's sack lunch.
10. **B and D taste great, but couldn't hit the fastball.**
11. The soccer-loving Brits might have trouble making sense of B or C.
12. **People in A and C spend a lot of time reading about B and D.**
13. Taking too big a chaw of A or D might make you B or C.
14. **Neither B nor D skates well, scores goals, or says "eh?"**
15. B and C never inspired much laughter in their day.
16. **You might get strange looks from a wrestler if you ask to see his B or C.**
17. You wouldn't want to hunt for A or D with a geologist who's B or C.
18. **At some point in their lives, A and C probably had to B or D.**
19. Though B is fictitious, it's somewhat believable. Even Calvin Klein wouldn't market C.
20. **If you tried to stay at A or D, their parents might get angry.**
21. It's quite possible that A and D have B or C.
22. **Some would consider it romantic to sit at a table in A or C and eat B or D.**
23. Though B and D aren't worth much, A and C don't even exist.
24. **Your kids might balk if you try to serve them B or C.**
25. You could win enough money from B or D to buy plenty of A and C.
26. **A tall bottle of Kirin or Asahi goes better with B and C.**
27. With the right map, you could actually visit A or C.
28. **You wouldn't want the nation's security in the hands of B or D.**
29. If you gave someone B or D, you would be very generous indeed; A and C are more realistic.
30. **If you had cooked A or C, you would have been put in jail.**
31. Hard-core drinkers wouldn't have much success tossing down B or D.
32. **Although all sound plausible, only B (Alabama) and C (Tulane) represent college teams.**
33. You couldn't find a box of B or C on the supermarket shelves.

34. **Run screaming from A and D; cheer loudly for B and C.**
35. A and D could do culinary wonders with B and C.
36. **A and C write good spots, but don't sing so hot.**
37. Believe it or not, you could do some shopping at A or D.
38. **A could sing C in B or D.**
39. Lewis Carroll dreamed up B and D, but A and C are alive and dangerous.
40. **You might get arrested if you tried to live on B or C.**
41. A and D were found in the sports pages; B and C in the comics.
42. **A Rastafarian would say B or C, and might eat A or D.**
43. B and D don't play much of a part in the Arthurian legends.
44. **B and D play well in the VCR; A and C play well in the clubs.**
45. All were judged, but only C and D involved boxers.
46. **Win money with B or C, take a trip to A or D.**
47. It would be quite a treat to see B and C swimming in A or D.
48. **Most people who live in A or D supported the appointments of B and C.**
49. A, C, and D are all in Maine, but only B and D are grown on farms.
50. **For good luck, you might try A or C before bombing down the slopes of B or D.**
51. B and D are orders; A and C are places you can visit.
52. **Buy B or C, then go listen to A and D.**
53. A (Randy Johnson) and C (Dennis Eckersley) are in the dugout; B and D are in the bedroom.

54. **Use B or D; live in A or C.**
55. Take a compact disc of C or D with you on your trip to A or B.
56. **A and C can really rock; B and D are fictional.**
57. Get on the bestsellers' list with B or D; get off the freeway at A or C.
58. **Eat A and C; run away if you hear B or D.**
59. Places in B and C serve A and D.
60. **Kickstart A and C; kick out the jams with B and D.**
61. Most men would rather watch A and C than play B or D.
62. **B and C are musical legends, and aren't considered A or D.**
63. Drink B and C while watching A or D miss a shot.
64. **Find B and C at your neighborhood store; you'd have to go further to find A and D.**
65. A and C stir the passions of European fans; B and D bore high school English students.
66. **You'll find stereos made by B and C in the dorm room of a student who is an A (Southern Illinois) or D (Georgetown).**
67. Upper-crust Britishers would know A and C, but might not have a clue about B or D.
68. **Add A and D to your food, B and C to the Austrian Davis Cup roster.**
69. "Fill 'er up" has a safer and more mundane meaning at A and D.
70. **Bruce and Demi could buy B or D to carry A and C.**
71. It's doubtful that A or B ever test-drove C or D.
72. **A, B, and D can hold four or five people, while A, B, and C can hold a few thousand more.**

73. The way B and C play ball, you might have more fun staying at home and paying your A and D bills.
74. **The jury's still out on whether you should fire C and D after drinking A or B.**
75. B tried to keep D from escaping, while A and C could just fly away.
76. **Deadheads love A and D, while B and C please different cults.**
77. Kirk and Spock dealt with B and C; Earth-bound people have A and D.
78. **Drink lots of B and C while listening to A and D.**
79. Priests in B and D say A and C.
80. **If you're not careful, a date after listening to B and D can result in a case of A or C.**
81. Farmers can work on B and D, and watch A or C.
82. **B (Minneapolis) and C (Beaumont) are old-time minor league teams.**
83. Small change will get you a copy of A or D.
84. **B or C can make your career; A and D can destroy you.**
85. Healthy teens dance to A and D.
86. **Don't look for A or D in a zoo or on "Wild Kingdom."**
87. People in A and C might not know the meaning of B or D.
88. **A and D get things really clean; B and C mop up on the field.**
89. Given a choice, men from Rio would take a night with A or B over a lesson in C or D.
90. **A and D don't exist; B and C are very real on the big screen.**

91. A, B, and C are done by European sportsmen; B, C, and D are done by European heavy drinkers.
92. **Read B and D, grind A and C.**
93. B could graduate from A; D could be a valedictorian at C.
94. **You notice A and C with your ears, B and D with your nose.**
95. Don't be offended if a friend offers you A or D.
96. **High school teachers mention A and B; their students thrash to C and D.**
97. A and C don't belong to a union; B and D probably couldn't rescue you from the evil empire.
98. **If you used B and C to help build a surfer's house, he might call you A or D.**
99. A did the singing, C played the drums, and they both ate B and D.
100. **People actually watched A and C.**
101. You'd be quite a celebrity if you had A or C in your pickup.
102. **Only a fool would have driven A or D to B or C.**
103. A and C probably didn't eat B or D before a big game.
104. **A and C have too much class to appear in B or D.**
105. B and D played in the majors; A and C you'll find on a map.
106. **No offense to A or D, but the signatures of B and C helped form our nation.**
107. A and D spend a lot of their time in the kitchen.
108. **A, B, and C all make sense to street jocks. A and D make sense to computer jocks.**
109. If a player has a tendency to B or D, he'll trade in his spikes for A or C.

110. **A and C could do a benefit concert for B or D.**
111. B and C play wide-open; A, B, and D help you play cautious.
112. **Get a great deal on a brand-new A or C.**
113. Drive downtown in your B or D to open A or C.
114. **Feel free to brag about your A or C, but you'd better keep quiet about your B or D.**
115. A or D didn't drink much B or C while constructing their masterpieces.
116. **A and C never held the esteemed office of the presidency.**
117. B and D were creepy; A and C were just plain wrong.
118. **A chess-playing A or C could find himself in B or D.**
119. A and B probably tipped a goblet or two of C or D.
120. **Fans smoked A, C, or D while watching A (Pittsburgh) and B (Newark) play.**
121. A and D are imaginary; too bad B and C aren't.
122. **Any European can visit A or C; only a select few can get through to B or D.**
123. It's hard to say which job is tougher, but A and C certainly got more respect than the hustling B or D.
124. **A and D can be bought with fake money; B and C aren't up for sale.**
125. You'd probably say A or C if you found yourself stuck in B or D.
126. **A and D are for your ears, B and C for your tastebuds.**
127. Cal Ripken, Jr., is neither A nor D, but he'll hit a B or C.
128. **Although B has left and C is dead, they helped build the Irish mystique.**

129. Although big dumb guys do all of these, B and D are relegated to big dumb guys who are pro wrestlers.
130. **Don't throw your can of A or bottle of C away while you hike in B or D.**
131. Miss Haversham wasn't too wild about B and D, but she might really be spooked by A and C.
132. **If you're Gorby, you don't want to see the name of A or C in the guest book. And, a little trick question for you: D fits both.**
133. Don't tell your peers that you're spending time with B and C to give yourself some style.
134. **If you ask your doctor if he has studied A or C, you'd better hope he's from Yoknapatawpha County, Mississippi.**
135. A and C were liars and cheats—*fictional* liars and cheats.
136. **If a modern-day monk is reading the works of B and D, he might consider going secular.**
137. If your AFS student starts requesting B or D, they've been in America too long.
138. **Cocktail party tip: Don't rave that B and D are brilliant, challenging, and artistic marvels.**
139. At least A and C won't keep you awake.
140. **An L.A. beach volleyball dude would think A and C are bitchin', but B and D are lame.**
141. A and C are generally used on boats; the others, generally are not.

142. **Cameron has yet to put Arnold up against B or D.**
143. If someone says you exude B or D, they might be calling you bankrupt.
144. **A and D have probably never been to Burbank.**
145. C and D never have their launch postponed by Mission Control.
146. **A and D's creator is a recluse; B and C's might want to think about it.**
147. It would have been a short trip if the explorer had eaten B or D when he was hungry.
148. **Hey, kids! Don't let your parents catch you doing A or D.**
149. Don't leave a tip with A or B, unless you really like your optometrist.
150. **You could go dancing at any of them, but you'd have a hard time finding the atomic weight of B and C.**
151. When the moon is doing B or D, aliens may have landed.
152. **Accusing someone of being A and B just means they're really old—*really* old.**
153. A and D wouldn't be a big draw in the zoo, unless it has a section for bureaucrats.
154. **John, Paul, George, and Ringo made lots of A and C from influence they picked up from B and D.**
155. The postal service wasn't great in those days, but B and D would be marked "return to sender."

156. **If you hung B and D in your home, you'd lose a few friends.**
157. A and D can last for a thousand years. B and C can start to give out after thirty.
158. **You can't get popcorn at A and D.**
159. When you hear A and C in your $100 Las Vegas seats, that's entertainment!
160. **Gomer would be wearing a turban if he uttered B or C.**
161. If they could find a CD player, they might listen to B and C in A and D.
162. **A and C had more weight and imagination than B and D.**
163. The work of A and C made possible a nation that reads B and D.
164. **If you're forced to defer to A or C, you don't have much seniority.**
165. The parties are better at B and D, unless you like discussing who rules the waves.
166. **A and C do a great job blocking, but B and D get all the glory.**
167. B might D and say "A (Not In My Back Yard)" to avoid a "C (Situation Normal All Fouled Up)."
168. **You might want to take A or C to get home to watch B and D.**
169. You can watch B or C with the set off.
170. **Banking with B or C would be interesting, or frustrating.**
171. B and D taste bad; A and C taste *terrible*.

172. **Taking the family to visit B and D might anger the groundskeeper.**
173. Hopefully, you won't find B and D at the Olympics.
174. **B and D had impressive lives, but they never hosted Gretzky.**
175. B and D are appropriate for young children; A and C are appropriate for people who like to bet a bundle.
176. **A and B blew wind; C and D blew smoke.**
177. You might see A or C on a channel transmitted on B or D.
178. **A and C might specialize in manifold meals.**
179. It's doubtful your local meteorologist would have a prediction regarding A or C.
180. **Rollercoasting is not in the official duties of A and C.**
181. If the baby is Russian (A) or German (C), then he might be a genius.
182. **You might B or D after A or C helps you catch the big one.**
183. The folks at A or C might rough up protesters, but they won't win the title doing it.
184. **Your spouse might hand you C or D if you watch too much A and B.**
185. If you packed up the U-Haul and moved to A or D, be sure to pack the popcorn.
186. **If you tell your partner you're going to show him B or D, it might be a long plane flight.**
187. A firm specializing in B or D might have a rocky time.

188. **A and C might have some horror scenes, but not on purpose.**
189. No, its not a trick question, even though A and C are a little on the geeky side.
190. **Don't flip your lighter for an encore at A or C.**
191. If you follow A or C, you're probably pretty smart; if you watched B or D, you're probably pretty dumb.
192. **B could have charmed his way onto the ticket, C could have frightened his way into the nomination, but Cary Grant and Boris Karloff chose acting instead.**
193. Although all are positive traits, A and C crushed the competition like bugs.
194. **Any state with B or D as their motto really likes Paul.**
195. You might find them all, if a crime had been committed against bees (A) and crows (C).
196. **The only discovery made by B and C has been comic obscurity.**
197. You might offend if you speak A or D.
198. **A close connection at A or C might require a meal of B or D.**
199. A mourns the death of C in the Bard's creation.
200. **You'll find B and D on the undesirable, not endangered, list.**